# THE

# GRIEVANCES

## OF THE

## American Colonies

### CANDIDLY EXAMINED.

'Midſt the low murmurs of ſubmiſſive Fear,
And mingled Rage, my HAMPDEN rais'd his voice,
And to the LAWS appeal'd.
                                    THOMSON.

Printed by AUTHORITY, at *Providence*, in
*Rhode-Iſland*.

## LONDON:

Reprinted for J. ALMON, oppoſite *Burlington-
Houſe*, in *Picadilly*. MDCCLXVI.

[ PRICE ONE SHILLING. ]

First Published 1766
Reprinted 1970

LIBRARY OF CONGRESS CATALOG CARD NUMBER:
70-124792

TO

THE RIGHT HONOURABLE

WILLIAM

EARL OF DARTMOUTH

FIRST LORD COMMISSIONER

OF THE

BOARD OF TRADE AND
PLANTATIONS:

THIS TRACT, LATELY PRINTED
BY AUTHORITY IN RHODE-ISLAND,

IS

MOST DUTIFULLY,

AND

MOST RESPECTFULLY
INSCRIBED.

# GRIEVANCES &c.

LIBERTY is the greatest blessing that men enjoy, and slavery the greatest curse that human nature is capable of.—Hence it is a matter of the utmost importance to men, which of the two shall be their Portion. Absolute liberty, is perhaps incompatible with any kind of government.—The safety resulting from society, and the advantage of just and equal laws, hath caused men to forego some part of their natural liberty, and submit to government. This appears to be the most rational account of its beginning; although it must be confessed, mankind have by no means been agreed about it: some have found its origin in the divine appointment;

B                               others

others have thought it took its rise from power: enthusiasts have dreamed that dominion was founded in grace. Leaving these points to be settled by the descendants of Filmer, Cromwell, and Venner, we shall consider the British constitution, as it at present stands, on Revolution Principles; and from thence endeavour to find the measure of the magistrate's power, and the people's obedience.

This glorious constitution, the best that ever existed amongst men, will be confessed by all, to be founded on compact, and established by consent of the people. By this most beneficent compact, British subjects are to be governed only agreeable to laws, to which themselves have some way consented, and are not to be compelled to part with their property, but as it is called for by the authority of such laws: the former is truly liberty; the latter is to be really possessed of property, and to have something that may be called one's own.

On

On the contrary, those who are governed at the will of another, or others, and whose Property may be taken from them by taxes, or otherwise, without their own consent, and against their will, are in the miserable condition of slaves: " For, (says Al-
" gernon Sidney, in his discourses on
" government) liberty solely consists
" in an independency upon the will
" of another; and by the name of
" slave, we understand a man who
" can neither dispose of his person or
" goods, but enjoys all at the will of
" his master." These things premised; whether the British American colonies on the continent, are justly entitled to like privileges and freedoms as their fellow subjects in Great Britain are, is a point worthy mature examination. In discussing this question, we shall make the colonies in New England, with whose rights we are best acquainted, the rule of our reasoning; not in the least doubting but all the others are justly entitled to like rights with them.

New

New England was firſt planted by adventurers, who left England, their native Country, by permiſſion of king Charles the firſt ; and at their own expence, tranſported themſelves to America, with great riſque and difficulty ſettled among ſavages, and in a very ſurprizing manner, formed new colonies in the wilderneſs. Before their departure, the terms of their freedom, and the relation they ſhould ſtand in to the mother country, in their emigrant ſtate were fully ſettled; they were to remain ſubject to the king, and dependant on the kingdom of Great Britain. In return they were to receive protection, and enjoy all the rights and privileges of freeborn Engliſhmen.

This is abundantly proved by the charter given to the Maſſachuſets colony, while they were ſtill in England, and which they received and brought over with them, as the authentic evidence of the conditions they removed upon. The colonies of Connecticut and

and Rhode Ifland alfo, afterwards
obtained charters from the crown,
granting them the like ample Privileges. By all thefe charters, it is in
the moft exprefs and folemn manner
granted, that thefe adventurers, and
their children after them for ever,
fhould have and enjoy all the freedom
and liberty that the fubjects in England enjoy : That they might make
laws for their own government, fuit-
able to their circumftances ; not re-
pugnant to, but as near as might be,
agreeable to the laws of England :
that they might purchafe lands, ac-
quire goods, and ufe trade for their
advantage, and have an abfolute property in whatever they juftly acquired.
Thefe, with many other gracious privileges, were granted them by feveral
Kings ; and they were to pay as an
acknowledgement to the crown, only
one fifth part of the ore of gold and
filver, that fhould at any time be found
in the faid colonies, in lieu of, and
full fatisfaction for all dues and de-
mands

mands of the crown and kingdom of England upon them.

There is not any thing new or extraordinary in thefe rights granted to the Britifh colonies :—The colonies from all countries, at all times, have enjoyed equal freedom with the mother ftate. Indeed, there would be found very few people in the world, willing to leave their native country, and go through the fatigue and hardfhip of planting in a new uncultivated one, for the fake of lofing their freedom. They who fettle new countries muft be poor ; and in courfe, ought to be free. Advantages, pecuniary or agreeable, are not on the Side of emigrants, and furely they muft have fomething in their ftead.

To illuftrate this, permit us to examine what hath generally been the condition of the colonies with refpect to their freedom; we will begin with thofe who went out from the ancient commonwealths of Greece, which are the firft perhaps, we have any good

good account of. Thucidides, that grave and judicious hiftorian, fays of one of them, " they were not fent " out to be flaves but to be the equals " of thofe who remained behind ;" and again, the Corinthians gave public notice, " that a new colony was " going to Epidamus, into which, all " that would enter, fhould have " equal and like privileges with thofe " who ftaid at home."

This was uniformly the condition of all the Grecian colonies ; they went out and fettled new countries ; they took fuch forms of government as themfelves chofe, though it generally nearly refembled that of the mother ftate, whether democratical or orligarchical. 'Tis true they were fond to acknowledge their original, and always oonfeffed themfelves under obligation to pay a kind of honorary refpect to, and fhew a filial dependance on the commonwealth from whence they fprung. Thucidides again tells us, that the Corinthians
complained

complained of the Coreyreans " from
" whom,though a colony of their own
" they had received some contemp-
" tuous treatment : for they neither
" payed them the usual honour on
" their public solemnities, nor began
" with a Corinthian in the distribu-
" tion of the sacrifices which is al-
" ways done by other colonies."
From hence it is plain what kind of
dependance the Greek colonies were
under, and what sort of acknowledgement they owed to the mother state.

If we pass from the Grecian to the
American colonies, we shall find
them not less free ; but this difference may be observed between them,
that the Roman colonies did not, like
the Grecian, become separate states,
governed by different laws, but always remained a part of the mother
state ; and all that were free of the
colonies, were also free of Rome.
And Grotius gives us the opinion of
a Roman king, concerning the freedom of Colonies : king Tullus says,
                              " for

" for our part, we look upon it to
" be neither truth nor juftice, that
" mother cities ought of neceffity,
" and by the law of nature, to rule
" over their colonies."

When we come down to the latter
ages of the world, and confider the
colonies planted in the three laft cen-
turies, in America, from feveral
kingdoms in Europe, we fhall find
them, fays Puffendorf, very different
from the antient colonies, and he gives
us an inftance in thofe of the Spa-
niards. Although it be confeffed thefe
fall greatly fhort of enjoying equal
freedom with the ancient Greek and
Roman ones ; yet it will be truly
faid, they enjoy equal freedom with
their countrymen in Spain : but as
they are all under the government of
an abfolute monarch, they have no
reafon to complain that one enjoys the
liberty the other is deprived of. The
French colonies will be found nearly
in the fame condition, and for the
fame reafon, becaufe their fellow-fub-

C                          jeels

jects of France have also loft their liberty. And the queftion is not whether all colonies, as compared with
one another, enjoy equal liberty, but
whether all enjoy as much freedom as
the inhabitants of the mother ftate ;
and this will hardly be denied in the
cafe of the Spanifh, French, or other
modern foreign colonies.

By this it fully appears, that colonies in general, both ancient and modern, have always enjoyed as much
freedom as the mother ftate from
which they went out : and will any
one fuppofe the Britifh colonies in
America are an exception to this general rule ? Colonies that came from
a kingdom renowned for liberty ;
from a conftitution founded on compact, from a people of all the fons of
men, the moft tenacious of freedom ;
who left the delights of their native
country, parted from their homes,
and all their conveniencies, fearched
out and fubdued a foreign country
with the moft amazing travail and
fortitude, to the infinite advantage and
emo-

emolument of the mother ftate ; that removed on a firm reliance of a folemn compact, and royal promife and grant, that they, and their fucceffors for ever, fhould be free, fhould be par- takers and fharers in all the privileges and advantages of the then Englifh, now Englifh conftitution.

If it were poffible a doubt could yet remain, in the moft unbeliev- ing mind, that thefe Britifh colo- nies are not every way juftly and fully intituled to equal liberty and freedom with their fellow-fubjects in Europe, we might fhew, that the parliament of Great-Britain have al- ways underftood their rights in the fame light.

By an act paffed in the thirteenth year of the reign of his late majefty King George the Second, intituled, " An act for naturalizing foreign pro- teftants, &c." and by another act, paffed in the fame reign, for nearly the fame purpofes, by both which it is enacted and ordained, " That all

foreign

" foreign proteſtants, who had in-
" habited, and reſided for the ſpace
" of ſeven years, or more, in His
" Majeſty's colonies in America,"
might, on the conditions therein
mentioned, be naturalized, and there-
upon ſhould be " deemed, adjudged,
" and taken to be His Majeſty's na-
" tural born ſubjeɔts of the kingdom
" of Great-Britain, to all intents,
" conſtruɔtions, and purpoſes, as if
" they, and every one of them, had
" been, or were born within the
" ſame." No reaſonable man will
here ſuppoſe the parliament intended,
in theſe aɔts, to put foreigners who
had been in the colonies only ſeven
years, in a better condition than thoſe
who had been born in them, or had
removed from Britain thither, but only to put theſe foreigners on an equa-
lity with them ; and, to do this, they
are obliged to give them all the rights
of natural-born ſubjeɔts of Great Britain.

From

From what has been shewn, it will appear beyond a doubt, that the British subjects in America, have equal rights with those in Britain; that they do not hold those rights as privileges granted them, but possess them as inherent and indefeasible.

And the British legislative and executive powers have considered the colonies as possessed of these rights, and have always heretofore, in the most tender and parental manner, treated them as their dependant (though free) condition required. The protection promised on the part of the crown, which with chearfulness and gratitude we acknowledge, hath at all times been given to the colonies. The dependance of the colonies to Great-Britain hath been fully testified by a constant and ready obedience to all the commands of His present Majesty, and royal predecessors; both men and money having been raised in them at all times when called for, with as much alacrity and in as large

pro-

proportions as hath been done in Great Britain, the ability of each confidered. It muft alfo be confef-fed with thankfulnefs, that the firft adventurers and their fucceffors, for one hundred and thirty years, have fully enjoyed all the freedoms and immunities promifed on their removal from England—But here the fcene feems to be unhappily changing :— The Britifh miniftry, whether induced by a jealoufy of the colonies, by falfe informations, or by fome altera-tion in the fyftem of political govern-ment, we have no information ; what-ever hath been the motive, this we are fure of, the parliament paffed an act, limitting reftricting, and bur-dening the trade of thofe colonies, much more than had ever been done before ; as alfo for greatly enlarging the power and jurifdiction of the Courts of admiralty in the colonies, and likewife paffed another act, efta-blifhing certain ftamp duties. Thefe acts have occafioned great uneafinefs
among

among the Britifh fubjects on the continent of America. How much reafon there is for it, we will endeavour,
in the moft modeft and plain manner
we can, to lay before the public.

In the firft place, let it be confidered, that although each of the colonies hath a legiflature within itfelf,
to take care of its Interefts, and pro-
vide for its peace and internal government, yet there are many things of
a more general nature, quite out of
the reach of thefe particular legifla-
tures, which it is neceffary fhould be
regulated, ordered and governed. One
of this kind is, the commerce of the
whole Britifh empire, taken collec-
tively, and that of each kingdom and
colony in it, as it makes a part of
that whole: Indeed, every thing that
concerns the proper intereft and fit
government of the whole commonwealth, of keeping the peace, and
fubordination of all the parts towards
the whole, and one among another,
muft be confidered in this light:
amongft

amongft thefe general concerns, perhaps money and paper credit, thofe
grand inftruments of all commerce,
will be found alfo to have a place.
Thefe, with all other matters of a
general nature, it is abfolutely neceffary fhould have a general power to
direct them; fome fupreme and over-
ruling authority, with power to make
laws, and form regulations for the
good of all, and to compel their execution and obfervation. It being
neceffary fome fuch general power
fhould exift fomewhere, every man
of the leaft knowledge of the Britifh conftitution, will be naturally
led to look for, and find it in the
parliament of Great Britain; that
grand and auguft legiflative body muft
from the nature of their authority,
and the neceffity of the thing, be
juftly vefted with this power. Hence
it becomes the indifpenfable duty of
every good and loyal fubject, chearfully to obey and patiently fubmit to
all the acts, laws, orders and regulations

tions that may be made and paſſed
by parliament, for directing and go-
verning all theſe general matters.

Here it may be urged by many,
and indeed, with great appearance of
reaſon, that the equity, juſtice and
beneficence, of the Britiſh conſtitu-
tion, will require, that the ſeparate
kingdoms and diſtinct colonies, who
are to obey and be governed by theſe
general laws and regulations, ought
to be repreſented, ſome way or other,
in parliament; at leaſt whilſt theſe
general matters are under conſider-
ation.   Whether the colonies will
ever be admitted to have repreſenta-
tives in parliament—whether it be
conſiſtent with their diſtant and dependant ſtate—and whether, if it
were admitted, it would be to their
advantage—are queſtions we will paſs
by ; and obſerve, that theſe colonies
ought in juſtice, and for the very
evident good of the whole commonwealth, to have notice of every new
meaſure about to be purſued,   and

new

new Act about to be pafled, by which their rights, liberties or interefts may be affected ; they ought to have fuch notice, that they may appear and be heard by their agents, by council, or written reprefentation, or by fome other equitable and effectual way.

The colonies are at fo great a diftance from England, that the members of parliament can, generally have but little knowledge of their bufinefs, connections and interefts, but what is gained from people who have been there ; the moft of thefe, have fo flight a knowledge themfelves, that the informations they can give, are very little to be depended on, though they may pretend to determine with confidence on matters far above their reach. All fuch informations are too uncertain to be depended on, in the tranfacting bufinefs of fo much confequence, and in which the interefts of

two

two millions of free people are fo
deeply concerned. There is no kind
of inconvenience or mifchief can arife
from the colonies having fuch notice,
and being heard in the manner above-
mentioned ; but, on the contrary,
very great mifchiefs have already hap-
pened to the colonies, and always
muft be expected, if they are not
heard, before things of fuch importance are determined concerning
them.

Had the colonies been fully heard,
before the late act had been paffed,
no reafonable man can fuppofe it ever
would have paffed at all, in the manner it now ftands ? for what good reafon can poffibly be given for making
a law to cramp the trade and ruin the
intereft of many of the colonies, and
at the fame time, leffen in a prodi-
gious manner the confumption of the
Britifh manufactures in them ? Thefe
are certainly the effects this act muft
produce : a duty of three-pence *per*
gallon on foreign melaffes, is well

known

known to every man in the leaſt acquainted with it, to be much higher
than that article can poſſibly bear ;
and therefore muſt operate as an abſolute prohibition. This will put a
total ſtop to the exportation of lumber, horſes, flour, and fiſh, to the
French and Dutch ſugar-colonies ;
and if any one ſuppoſe we may find a
ſufficient vent for theſe articles in the
Engliſh Weſt-Indies, he only verifies
what was juſt now obſerved, that he
wants true information. Putting an
end to the importation of foreign melaſſes, at the ſame time puts an end
to all the coſtly diſtilleries in theſe
colonies, and to the rum trade with
the coaſt of Africa, and throws it into the Hands of the French. With
the loſs of the foreign melaſſes trade,
the cod-fiſhery in America muſt alſo
be loſt, and thrown alſo into the hands
of the French. That this is the real
ſtate of the whole buſineſs is not mere
fancy ; neither this, nor any part of
it,

it, is exaggeration, but a fober and moft melancholy truth.

View this duty of three-pence *per* gallon on foreign melaffes, not in the light of a prohibition, but fuppofing the trade to continue, and the duty to be paid. Heretofore there hath been imported into the colony of Rhode-Ifland only, about one million one hundred and fifty thoufand gallons, annually ; the duty on this quantity is fourteen thoufand three hundred and feventy-five pounds fterling, to be paid yearly by this little colony; a larger fum than was ever in it at any one time. This money is to be fent away, and never to return ; yet the payment is to be repeated every year. —Can this poffibly be done ? Can a new colony, compelled by neceffity to purchafe all its cloathing, furniture, and utenfils from England, to fupport the expences of its own internal go-vernment, obliged by its duty to com-ply with every call from the crown to raife money on emergencies ; after all this,

this, can every man in it pay twen-
ty-four fhillings a year for the duties
of a fingle article only ; There is
furely no man in his right mind be-
lieves this poffible. The charging foreign melaffes with this high duty,
will not affect all the colonies equally,
nor any other near fo much as this of
Rhode-ifland, whofe trade depended
much more on foreign melaffes, and
on diftilleries, than that of any others;
this muft fhew that raifing money
for the general fervice of the crown,
or colonies, by fuch a duty, will be
extremely unequal, and therefore un-
juft.   And now taking either alterna-
tive ;  by fuppofing, on one hand, the
foreign melaffes trade is ftopped, and
with it the opportunity or ability of
the colonies to get money ;  or, on
the other, that this trade is continued,
and that the colonies get money by it,
but all their money is taken from
them by paying their duty ;  can Britain be a gainer by either ? Is it not
the chief intereft of Britain to difpofe
of,

of, and be paid for her own manufactures? and doth she not find the greatest and best market for them in her own colonies? Will she find an advantage in disabling the colonies to continue their trade with her? or can she possibly grow rich by their being made poor?

Ministers have great influence, and parliaments have great power;—can either of them change the nature of things, stop our means of getting money, and yet expect us to purchase and pay for British manufactures? The genius of the people in these colonies is as little turned to manufacturing goods for their own use, as is possible to suppose in any people whatsoever; yet necessity will compel them either to go naked in this cold country, or to make themselves some sort of cloathing, if it be only of the skins of Beasts.

By the same act of parliament, the exportation of all kinds of timber, or lumber, the most natural
produce

produce of thefe new colonies, is greatly incumbered and ufelefsly em-barraffed, and the fhipping it to any part of Europe, except Great Britain, prohibited : This muft greatly affect the linen manufacture in Ireland, as that kingdom ufed to receive great quantities of flax-feed from America, many cargoes being made of that, and of barrel ftaves, were fent thither every year ; but as the ftaves can no longer be exported thither, the fhips carrying only flax feed cafks, with-out the ftaves, which ufed to be in-termixed among them, muft lofe one half of their freight, which will pre-vent their continuing this trade, to the great injury of Ireland, and of the plantations : And what advantage is to accrue to Great Britain by it, muft be told by thofe who can per-ceive the utility of this meafure.

Enlarging the power and jurifdic-tion of the courts of vice-admiralty in the colonies, is another part of the fame act, greatly and juftly complained

of

of. Courts of admiralty have long
been eftablifhed in moft of the colonies, whofe authority were circum-
fcribed within moderate territorial ju-
rifdictions ; and whofe courts have
always done the Bufinefs neceffary to
be brought before thofe courts for
trial, in the manner it ought to be
done, and in a way only moderately
expenfive to the fubjects ; and if
feizures were made, or informations
exhibited, without reafon, or contrary to law, the informer or feizer,
was left to the juftice of the com-
mon law, there to pay for his folly,
or fuffer for his temerity. But now
this cafe is quite altered, and a cuf-
tom houfe officer may make a feizure
in Georgia, of goods ever fo legally
imported, and carry the trial to Ha-
lifax, at fifteen hundred miles diftance,
and thither the owner muft follow
him to defend his property ; and when
he comes there, quite beyond the cir-
cle of his friends, acquaintance, and
correfpondence, among total ftrangers,

E                                    he

he muſt there give bond, and muſt
find ſureties to be bound with him in
a large ſum before he ſhall be admitted to claim his own goods ; when
this is complied with, he hath a trial,
and his goods acquitted. If the judge
can be prevailed on (which it is very
well known may too eaſily be done) to
certify, there was *only* probable cauſe
for making the ſeizure, the unhappy
owner can not maintain any action
againſt the illegal ſeizer, for damages,
or obtain any ſatisfaction ; but he may
return to Georgia, quite ruined, and
undone in conformity to an act of
parliament. Such unbounded encou-
ragement and protection given to informers, muſt call to every one's re-
membrance Tacitus's account of the
miſerable condition of the Romans
in the reign of Tiberius their emperor, who let looſe and encouraged the
informers of that age. Surely if the
colonies had been fully heard before
this had been done, the liberties and
properties

properties of the Americans would not have been so much disregarded.

The resolution that the house of commons came into during the same session of parliament, asserting their right to establish stamp duties, and internal taxes, to be collected in the colonies without their own consent, hath much more, and for much more reason alarmed the British subjects in America, than any thing that had ever been done before. These resolutions have been since carried into execution by an act of parliament which the colonists do conceive is a violation of their long enjoyed rights. For it must be confessed by all men, that they who are taxed at Pleasure by others, cannot possibly have any property, can have nothing to be called their own; they who have no property can have no freedom, but are indeed reduced to the most abject slavery; are in a state far worse than countries conquered and made tributary; for these have only a fixed sum

to

to pay, which they are left to raife among themfelves, in the way that they may think moft equal and eafy; and having paid the ftipulated fum, the debt is difcharged, and what is left is their own. This is more tolerable, than to be taxed at the mere will of others, without any bounds, without any ftipulation or agreement, contrary to their confent and againft their wills. If we are told that thofe who lay thefe taxes upon the colonies are men of the higheft character for wifdom juftice and integrity, and therefore cannot be fuppofed to deal hardly, unjuftly or unequally by any; admitting, and really believing that all this is true, it will make no alteration in the nature of the cafe; for one who is bound to obey the will of another, is as really a flave, though he may have a good mafter, as if he had a bad one; and this is ftronger in politic bodies than in natural ones, as the former have a perpetual fucceffion, and remain the fame; and

although

although they may have a good mafter at one time, they may have a
very bad one at another. And indeed,
if the people in America, are to be
taxed by the reprefentatives of the
people in Britain, their malady is an
increafing evil, that muft always grow
greater by time. Whatever burdens
are laid upon the Americans, will be
fo much taken off the Britons ; and
the doing this will foon be extremely popular, and thofe who put up to
be members of the houfe of commons, muft obtain the votes of
the people, by promifing to take
taxes off them, by making new
levies on the Americans. This muft
moft affuredly be the cafe, and it
will not be in the power even of
the parliament to prevent it ; the
people's private intereft will be concerned, and will govern them ; they
will have fuch, and only fuch reprefentatives as will act agreeable to
their intereft ; and thefe taxes, laid
on Americans, will be always a part
of

of the fupply bill, in which the other branches of the legiflature can make no alteration : and, in truth, the fub-jects in the colonies will be taxed at the will and pleafure of their fellow-fubjects in Britain.——How equitable and how juft this may be, muft be left to every impartial man to deter-mine.

But it will be faid, that the monies drawn from the colonies by duties, and by taxes, will be laid up and fet apart to be ufed for their future de-fence : this will not at all alleviate the hardfhip, but ferve only more ftrongly to mark the fervile ftate of the people. Free people have ever thought, and always will think, that the money neceffary for their defence, lies fafeft in their own hands, until it be wanted immediately for that pur-pofe. To take the money of the A-mericans, which they want continu-ally to ufe in their trade, and lay it up for their defence, at a thoufand leagues diftant from them, when the

enemies

enemies they have to fear are in their own neighbourhood, hath not the greateſt probability of friendſhip or of prudence.

It is not the judgment of free people only, that money for defend-ing them is ſafeſt in their keeping, but it is alſo the opinion of the beſt and wiſeſt kings and governors of mankind, in every age of the world, that the wealth of a ſtate was moſt ſecurely as well as moſt profitably depoſited in the hands of their faith-ful ſubjects : Conſtantius, emperor of the Romans, though an abſolute prince, both practiſed and praiſed this method. "Dioclefian ſent per-"ſons on purpoſe to reproach him "with his neglect of the publick, "and the poverty to which he was "reduced by his own fault. Con-"ſtantius heard theſe reproaches "with patience; and having per-"ſuaded thoſe who made them in "Dioclefian's name, to ſtay a few "days with him, he ſent word to
"the

" the moſt wealthy perſons in the
" provinces, that he wanted money,
" and that they had now an oppor-
" tunity of ſhewing whether or no
" they really loved their prince. Up-
" on this notice, every one ſtrove
" who ſhouid be foremoſt in carry-
" ing to the exchequer all their gold,
" ſilver, and valuable effects, ſo that
" in a ſhort time, Conſtantius from
" being the pooreſt, became by far
" the moſt wealthy of all the four
" princes. He then invited the de-
" puties of Diocleſian to viſit his
" treaſury, deſiring them to make a
" faithful report to their maſter of
" the ſtate in which they ſhould
" find it. They obeyed ; and, while
" they ſtood gazing upon the migh-
" ty heaps of gold and ſilver, Con-
" ſtantius told them, that the wealth
" which they beheld with aſtoniſh-
" ment, had long ſince belonged to
" him, but that he had left it by
" way of depoſitum, in the hands
" of his people: adding, the richeſt
                                    " and

" and fureft treafure of the prince,
" was the love of his fubjects. The
" deputies were no fooner gone,
" than the generous prince fent for
" thofe who had affifted him in his
" exigency, commended their zeal
" and returned to every one what
" they had fo readily brought into
" his treafury."

We are not infenfible, that when
liberty is in danger, the liberty of
complaining is dangerous; yet a man
on a wrack was never denied the liberty of roaring as loud as he could,
fays Dean Swift. And we believe no
good reafon can be given, why the
colonies fhould not modeftly and fo-
berly enquire, what right the parliament of Great Britain have to tax
them. We know that fuch enquiries
have by one letter writer, been brand-
ed with the little epithet of *Mufh-
room Policy* ; and he intimates, that
for the colonies to pretend to claim
any privileges, will draw down the
refentment of the parliament on

F                         them

them. Is then the defence of liberty become so contemptible, and pleading for juft rights fo dangerous? Can the guardians of liberty be thus ludicrous? Can the patrons of freedom be fo jealous and fo fevere?

Should it be urged that the money expended by the mother-country, for the defence and protection of America, and efpecially during the late war, muft juftly entitle her to fome retaliation from the colonies; and that the ftamp duties and taxes, intended to be raifed in them, are only defigned for that equitable purpofe; if we are permitted to examine how far this may rightfully veft the parliament with the power of taxing the colonies, we fhall find this claim to have no foundation. In many of the colonies, efpecially thofe in New England, which were planted, as is before obferved, not at the charge of the crown or kingdom of England, but at the expence of the planters themfelves, and were

not

not only planted, but also defended
against the savages and other enemies,
in long and cruel wars, which continued for an hundred years, almost
without intermission, solely at their
own charge : and in the year 1746,
when the Duke d'Anville came out
from France, with the most formida-
ble French fleet that ever was in the
American seas, enraged at these colonies for the loss of Louisbourg the
year before, and with orders to make
an attack on them ; even in this
greatest exigence, these colonies were
left to the protection of heaven, and
their own efforts. These colonies
having thus planted and defended
themselves, and removed all enemies
from their borders, were in hopes to
enjoy peace, and recruit their state,
much exhausted by these long strug-
gles ; but they were soon called upon
to raise men, and send them out to the
defence of other colonies, and to make
conquests for the crown ; they dutifully obeyed the requisition, and with

ardour

ardour entered into thofe ferviccs, and
continued in them until all encroach-
ments were removed, and all Canada,
and even the Havannah conquered.
They moft chearfully complied with
every call of the crown; they re-
joiced, yea even exulted in the pro-
fperity of the Britifh empire. But
thefe colonies whofe bounds were
fixed, and whofe borders were before
cleared from enemies, by their own
fortitude, and at their own expence,
reaped no fort of advantage by thefe
conquefts; they are not enlarged,
have not gained a fingle acre of land,
have no part in the Indian or interior
trade; the immenfe tracts of land
fubdued, and no lefs immenfe and
profitable commerce acquired, all be-
long to Great-Britain; and not the
leaft fhare or portion to thefe colonies,
though thoufands of their members
have loft their lives, and millions of
their money have been expended in
the purchafe of them; for great part
of which we are yet in debt, and
from

from which we fhall not in many years be able to extricate ourfelves. Hard will be the fate, cruel the deftiny of thefe unhappy colonies, if the reward they are to receive for all this is the lofs of their freedom ; better for them Canada ftill remained French, yea far more eligible that it ever fhould remain fo, than that the price of its reduction fhould be their flavery.

If the colonies are not taxed by parliament, are they therefore exempted from bearing their proper fhares in the neceffary burdens of government ? This by no means follows. Do they not fupport a regular internal government in each colony, as expenfive to the people here, as the internal government of Britain is to the people there ? Have not the colonies here, at all times when called upon by the crown to raife money for the public fervice, done it as chearfully as the parliament have done on the like occafions ? Is not this the

most

moſt eaſy way of raiſing money in the
colonies? What occaſion then to dif-
truſt the colonies, what neceſſity to
fall on the preſent method to compel
them to do what they have ever
done freely? Are not the people in
the colonies as loyal and dutiful ſubjects as any age or nation ever pro-
duced,—and are they not as uſeful
to the kingdom in this remote quar-
ter of the world, as their fellow-ſub-
jects are in Britain? The parliament,
it is confeſſed, have power to regu-
late the trade of the whole empire;
and hath it not full power, by this
means, to draw all the money and
wealth of the colonies into the mother
country, at pleaſure? What motive,
after all this can remain, to induce the
parliament to abridge the privileges,
and leſſen the rights of the moſt loyal
and dutiful ſubjects; ſubjects juſtly
intitled to ample freedom, who have
long enjoyed, and not abuſed or fot-
feited their liberties, who have uſed
them to their own advantage, in dutiful

tiful fubferviency to the orders and the interefts of Great-Britain ? Why fhould the gentle current of tranquility, that has fo long run with peace through all the Britifh ftates, and flowed with joy and with happinefs in all her countries, be at laft obftructed, and turned out of its true courfe, into unufual and winding channels, by which many of thefe colonies muft be ruined ; but none of them can poffibly be made more rich or more happy.

Before we conclude, it may be neceffary to take notice of the vaft difference there is between the raifing money in a country by duties, taxes, or otherwife, and employing and laying out the money again in the fame country ; and raifing the like fums of money, by the like means, and fending it away quite out of the country where it is raifed. Where the former of thefe is the cafe, although the fums raifed may be very great, yet that country may fupport itfelf under
them ;

them ; for as faft as the money is collected together, it is again fcattered
abroad, to be ufed in commerce and
every kind of bufinefs, and money is
not made fcarcer by this means, but
rather the contrary, as this continual
circulation muft have a tendency, in
fome degree, to prevent its being
hoarded. But where the latter method is purfued, the effect will be extremely different; for here, as faft as
the money can be collected, it is immediately fent out of the country,
never to return but by a tedious round
of commerce, which at beft muft take
up much time: here all trade, and
every kind of bufinefs depending upon
it will grow dull, and muft languifh
more and more, until it comes to a
final ftop at laft. If the money raifed in Great-Britain in the three laft
years of the late war, and which ex-
ceeded forty millions fterling, had
been fent out of the kingdom, would
not this have nearly ruined the trade
of the nation in three years only?
Think

Think then what muſt be the condition of theſe miſerable colonies, when
all the money propoſed to be raiſ-
ed in them, by high duties on the
importation of divers kinds of goods,
by the poſt-office, by ſtamp-duties.
and other taxes, is ſent quite away,
as faſt as it can be collected : and this
is to be repeated continually ! Is it
poſſible for colonies under theſe cir-
cumſtances to ſupport themſelves, to
have any money, any trade, or other
buſineſs carried on in them ? Certainly it is not ; nor is there at preſent,
or ever was, any country under heaven, that did, or poſſibly could ſupport itſelf under ſuch burdens.

We finally beg leave to aſſert that
the firſt planters of theſe colonies
were pious Chriſtians, were faithful
ſubjects : who, with a fortitude and
perſeverance little known, and leſs
conſidered, ſettled theſe wild countries, by God's goodneſs and their
own amazing labours ; thereby added

G                    a moſt

a moſt valuable dependance to the crown of Great-Britain, were ever dutifully ſubſervient to her intereſts; they ſo taught their children, that not one has been diſaffected to this day, but all have honeſtly obeyed every royal command, and chearfully ſubmitted to every conſtitutional law; they have as little inclination as they have ability to throw off their dependancy: they have moſt carefully avoided every meaſure that might be offenſive, and all ſuch manufactures as were interdicted. Beſides all this, they have riſked their lives when they have been ordered, and furniſhed their money whenever it has been called for; have never been either troubleſome or expenſive to the mother country; have kept all due order, and have ſupported a regular government; they have maintained peace, and practiſed Chriſtianity. And in all conditions, upon all occasions, and in every relation, they have always demeaned themselves as loyal, as dutiful subjects ought to do : and no kingdom, or state, or empire, hath, or ever had colonies more quiet, or more obedient, more serviceable, more profitable than these have ever been.

May the same Divine Goodness, that guided the first Planters, that protected the settlements, and inspired Kings to be gracious, Parliaments to be tender ; ever preserve, ever protect and support our present Most Gracious King ; give great wisdom to his ministrrs, and much understanding to his parliament ; perpetuate the sovereignty of the British constitution, and the filial dependancy of all the colonies.

*Providence, in New-England.*

77859